2016

Microsoft Outlook Shortcut – A Rapid Reference
Over 345 Rarely Known and Used Outlook Shortcuts

Sushi

Tiny Publications

TABLE OF CONTENTS

INTRODUCTION

Microsoft Outlook email client application is a leading email and collaboration tool from Microsoft Corporation. As an Outlook user you would already be aware that Microsoft office application and most of similar office applications requires extensive use of keyboard. However, it tend to be very annoying when you must take your hands off the keyboard and perform some very trivial job such as click Reply, Forward, checking new emails, inserting attachments, sending email, and so on. Moreover, if you need to work on a large number of emails it could be a very frustrating experience at times.

However, not many of us know that a number of applications on Windows platform come with a bunch of shortcuts that may be used to invoke a functionality or features in such application. Microsoft Outlook 2013 alone has more than 300 shortcut key sequences. These shortcuts are hardly known to an average email user. It would not be an exaggeration to state that not more than 5% of outlook user base can really claim that they know the application in true sense of the term.

This reference guide contains all the shortcuts discovered, which may or may not have been documented. Knowing and using these shortcuts can make you a pro Outlook user beyond all doubts.

I would like to state it categorically here that, to use the Microsoft Outlook application it is not at a requirement to know any particular shortcut key. The application has been designed beautifully to help you easily navigate the application without any knowledge. However, if you do not know the computer shortcuts and/or do not to use shortcuts you may not be able to work at the same speed and accuracy as another user who knows and uses shortcut keys.

WHAT IS A SHORTCUT?

On the computer keyboard, a combination or sequence of key strokes that is used to invoke a command, or an action to perform a pre-defined task or to produce a pre-defined result or output through a computer software or program can be termed as a keyboard shortcut. Thus, a shortcut could potentially be

- A single key (often known as hotkey e.g. Function Keys F1 through F12)
- A key combination
- A key sequence

Every shortcut must invoke a pre-configured functionality or action. When a sequence of keys is configured as a shortcut, in most of the cases it requires pressing and holding down at least one key and then pressing and releasing a key or a set of keys in a certain sequence. The key that you must press and hold is called as a "**Modifier**" key. As a rule of thumb you only need to press the modifier key and continue to keep it holding until all keys in the key sequence are pressed and released in the specified sequence.

INTERPRETING SHORTCUTS

As a rule of thumb, most of the shortcut key combinations are likely to require pressing one or more of modifier keys such as **Alt, Ctrl, Shift, Win,** or **Command** Key (in case of Apple Computer Systems). The shortcut key is usually completed with a one or more set of keys. Unless otherwise specified you will need to press the keys in the same sequence to get the results mentioned in this eBook.

This eBook follows the de facto standard used in writing shortcut key strokes in documentation, or computer software help files and product manuals. In the following sections you will find shortcut listing made up of a modifier key (**Alt, Shift, Ctrl, Win,** or **Command** key), a plus symbol (+), and single or a set of character key combinations. For instance, a shortcut reading **Ctrl + K** should be interpreted to press and hold **Ctrl** key and press the **K** key. It is important to make note here that when you press the modifier key you must continue to press and hold it until you hit the second key in the key-sequence.

In case of a shortcut that requires you to press more than two keys, in some cases you may be able to leave the modifier key while in other case you will have to keep it holding. It depends on the application and situation. Similarly, in such multi-key shortcuts the key presses may need to be in quick sequence.

MICROSOFT OUTLOOK SHORTCUT KEYS

Microsoft Outlook is a personal information manager from Microsoft. It is available both as a part of the Microsoft Office suite and also as a standalone application program. Microsoft Outlook is often used mainly as an e-mail Application. It also includes a calendar, task manager, contact manager, note taking, a journal and web browsing. The current version is Microsoft Outlook 2013 for Windows and 2011 for Mac.

Below is a listing of all the major shortcut keys in Microsoft Outlook. There are generic outlook shortcuts. See the computer shortcut page if you are looking for other shortcut keys used in other programs.

Shortcut Keys	Assigned Action
Alt + S	Send the e-mail
Ctrl + C	Copy selected text.
Ctrl + X	Cut selected text.
Ctrl + P	Print selected text.
Ctrl + K	Complete the name or e-mail being typed in the e-mail address bar.
Ctrl + B	Bold highlighted selection
Ctrl + I	Italic highlighted selection

Ctrl + M	Send and receive all
Ctrl + U	Underline highlighted selection
Ctrl + R	Reply to an e-mail.
Ctrl + F	Forward an e-mail.
Ctrl + N	Create a new e-mail.
Ctrl + Y	Go to folder.
Ctrl + Shift + A	Create a new appointment to your calendar.
Ctrl + Shift + O	Open the Outbox.
Ctrl + Shift + I	Open the Inbox.
Ctrl + Shift + K	Add a new task.
Ctrl + Shift + C	Create a new contact.
Ctrl + Shift + J	Create a new journal entry.
Ctrl + Shift + V	Move folder

Table 12

MICROSOFT OFFICE - OUTLOOK 2013 KEYBOARD SHORTCUTS

Following shortcuts apply to MS-Outlook 2013. Many of them are backward compatible and therefore can be used an almost all version of MS-Outlook. For readers convenience we have compiled them under appropriate sections such as search, navigation, email etc.

USER INTERFACE NAVIGATION

Shortcut Keys	Assigned Action
CTRL+1	Switch to Mail view
CTRL+2	Switch to Calendar view
CTRL+3	Switch to Contacts view
CTRL+4	Switch to Tasks view
CTRL+5	Switch to Notes view

CTRL+6	Switch to Folder List in Navigation Pane.
CTRL+7	Switch to Shortcuts
CTRL+PERIOD	Switch to next message (when current email message is open in a separate window)
CTRL+COMMA	Switch to previous message (when current email message is open in a separate window)
F6 **or** **CTRL+SHIFT+TAB**	Move between the Navigation Pane, the main Outlook window, the Reading Pane, and the To-Do Bar.
TAB	Move between the Outlook window, the smaller panes in the Navigation Pane, the Reading Pane, and the sections in the To-Do Bar.
Arrow keys	Move around within the Navigation Pane.
CTRL+Y	Go to a different folder.
F3 or CTRL+E	Go to the Search box.
ALT+UP ARROW or CTRL+COMMA or ALT+PAGE UP	In the Reading Pane, go to the previous message.
SPACEBAR	In the Reading Pane, page down through text.
SHIFT+SPACEBAR	In the Reading Pane, page up through text.
SHIFT+PLUS SIGN	Expand a group (with a group selected) in the Navigation Pane.
SHIFT+ MINUS SIGN	Collapse a group (with a group selected) in the Navigation Pane.
LEFT ARROW or RIGHT ARROW, respectively	Collapse or expand a group in the e-mail message list.
SHIFT+TAB	Move to next field in Reading Pane.
CTRL+TAB	Move to previous field in Reading Pane.
ALT+B, ALT+LEFT ARROW, or ALT+BACKSPACE	Go back to previous view in main Outlook window.
ALT+RIGHT ARROW	Go forward to next view in main Outlook window.

CTRL+SHIFT+W	Select the InfoBar and, if available, show the menu of commands.

SEARCH

Press	Assigned Action
CTRL+E	Find a message or other item.
ESC	Clear the search results.
CTRL+ALT+A	Expand the search to include All Mail Items, All Calendar Items, or All Contact Items, depending on the module you are in.
CTRL+ALT+W	Expand the Search Query Builder.
CTRL+SHIFT+F	Use Advanced Find.
CTRL+SHIFT+P	Create a new Search Folder.
F4	Search for text within a message or other item.
SHIFT+F4	Find next during text search within a message or other item.
CTRL+H	Find and replace text, symbols, or some formatting commands within open items. Works in the Reading Pane on an open item.
CTRL+ALT+K	Expand search to include the desktop.

FLAGS

Shortcut Keys	Assigned Action
CTRL+SHIFT+G	Open the Flag for Follow Up dialog box to assign a flag.

COLOR CATEGORIES

Shortcut Keys	Assigned Action
ALT+D	Delete the selected category from the list in the Color Categories dialog box.

CREATE AN ITEM OR FILE

Shortcut Keys	Assigned Action
CTRL+SHIFT+A	Create an appointment.

CTRL+SHIFT+C	Create a contact.
CTRL+SHIFT+L	Create a distribution list.
CTRL+SHIFT+X	Create a fax.
CTRL+SHIFT+E	Create a folder.
CTRL+SHIFT+J	Create a Journal entry.
CTRL+SHIFT+Q	Create a meeting request.
CTRL+SHIFT+M	Create a message.
CTRL+SHIFT+N	Create a note.
CTRL+SHIFT+H	Create a new Microsoft Office document.
CTRL+SHIFT+S	Post to this folder.
CTRL+T	Post a reply in this folder.
CTRL+SHIFT+P	Create a Search Folder.
CTRL+SHIFT+K	Create a task.
CTRL+SHIFT+U	Create a task request.

ALL ITEMS

Shortcut Keys	Assigned Action
CTRL+S or SHIFT+F12	Save.
ALT+S	Save and close.
F12	Save as.
CTRL+Z or ALT+BACKSPACE	Undo.
CTRL+D	Delete an item.
CTRL+P	Print.
CTRL+SHIFT+Y	Copy an item.
CTRL+SHIFT+V	Move an item.
CTRL+K	Check names.
F7	Check spelling.

CTRL+SHIFT+G	Flag for follow-up.
CTRL+F	Forward.
ALT+S	Send or post or invite all.
F2	Turn on editing in a field (except in Icon view).
CTRL+L	Left align text.
CTRL+E	Center text.
CTRL+R	Right align text.

E-MAIL

Shortcut Keys	Assigned Action
CTRL+SHIFT+I	Switch to Inbox.
CTRL+SHIFT+O	Switch to Outbox.
CTRL+TAB (with focus on the To box) and then TAB to the Accounts button	Choose the account from which to send a message.
CTRL+K	Check names.
ALT+S	Send.
CTRL+R	Reply to a message.
CTRL+SHIFT+R	Reply all to a message.
CTRL+F	Forward a message.
CTRL+ ALT+J	Mark a message as not junk.
CTRL+SHIFT+I	Display blocked external content (in a message).
CTRL+ SHIFT+S	Post to a folder.
CTRL+SHIFT+N	Apply Normal style.
CTRL+M or F9	Check for new messages.
UP ARROW	Go to the previous message.
DOWN ARROW	Go to the next message.

CTRL+N	Create a new message (when in Mail).
CTRL+SHIFT+M	Create a new message (from any Outlook view).
CTRL+O	Open a received message.
CTRL+SHIFT+B	Open the Address Book.
CTRL+SHIFT+O	Convert an HTML or RTF message to plain text.
INSERT	Add a Quick Flag to an unopened message.
CTRL+SHIFT+G	Display the Flag for Follow Up dialog box.
CTRL+Q	Mark as read.
CTRL+U	Mark as unread.
CTRL+SHIFT+W	Show the menu to download pictures, change automatic download settings, or add a sender to the Safe Senders List.
F4	Find or replace.
SHIFT+F4	Find next.
CTRL+ENTER	Send.
CTRL+P	Print.
CTRL+F	Forward.
CTRL+ALT+F	Forward as attachment.
ALT+ENTER	Show the properties for the selected item.
CTRL+ALT+M	Mark for Download.
CTRL+ALT+U	Clear Mark for Download.
CTRL+B (when a Send/Receive is in progress)	Display Send/Receive progress.

CALENDAR

Shortcut Keys	Assigned Action
CTRL+N	Create a new appointment (when in

	Calendar).
CTRL+SHIFT+A	Create a new appointment (in any Outlook view).
CTRL+SHIFT+Q	Create a new meeting request.
CTRL+F	Forward an appointment or meeting.
CTRL+R	Reply to a meeting request with a message.
CTRL+SHIFT+R	Reply All to a meeting request with a message.
ALT+0	Show 10 days in the calendar.
ALT+1	Show 1 day in the calendar.
ALT+2	Show 2 days in the calendar.
ALT+3	Show 3 days in the calendar.
ALT+4	Show 4 days in the calendar.
ALT+5	Show 5 days in the calendar.
ALT+6	Show 6 days in the calendar.
ALT+7	Show 7 days in the calendar.
ALT+8	Show 8 days in the calendar.
ALT+9	Show 9 days in the calendar.
CTRL+G	Go to a date.
ALT+= or CTRL+ALT+4	Switch to Month view.
CTRL+RIGHT ARROW	Go to the next day.
ALT+DOWN ARROW	Go to the next week.
ALT+PAGE DOWN	Go to the next month.
CTRL+LEFT ARROW	Go to the previous day.
ALT+UP ARROW	Go to the previous week.
ALT+PAGE UP	Go to the previous month.
ALT+HOME	Go to the start of the week.

ALT+END	Go to the end of the week.
ALT+MINUS SIGN or CTRL+ALT+3	Switch to Full Week view.
CTRL+ALT+2	Switch to Work Week view.
CTRL+COMMA or CTRL+SHIFT+COMMA	Go to previous appointment.
CTRL+PERIOD or CTRL+SHIFT+PERIOD	Go to next appointment.
CTRL+G	Set up recurrence for an appointment or task.

CONTACTS

Shortcut Keys	Assigned Action
CTRL+SHIFT+D	Dial a new call.
F3 or CTRL+E	Find a contact or other item.
F11	Enter a name in the Search Address Books box.
SHIFT+letter	In Table or List view of contacts, go to first contact that starts with a specific letter.
CTRL+A	Select all contacts.
CTRL+F	Create a new message addressed to selected contact.
CTRL+J	Create a Journal entry for the selected contact.
CTRL+N	Create a new contact (when in Contacts).
CTRL+SHIFT+C	Create a new contact (from any Outlook view).
CTRL+O or CTRL+SHIFT+ENTER	Open a contact form for the selected contact.
CTRL+SHIFT+L	Create a new distribution list.
CTRL+P	Print.
F5	Update a list of distribution list members.
CTRL+Y	Go to a different folder.
CTRL+SHIFT+B	Open the Address Book.
CTRL+SHIFT+F	Use Advanced Find.

CTRL+SHIFT+PERIOD	In an open contact, open the next contact listed.
ESC	Close a contact.
CTRL+SHIFT+X	Open a Web page for the selected contact (if one is included).
ALT+D	Open the Check Address dialog box.
ALT+SHIFT+1	In a contact form, under Internet, display the E-mail 1 information.
ALT+SHIFT+2	In a contact form, under Internet, display the E-mail 2 information.
ALT+SHIFT+3	In a contact form, under Internet, display the E-mail 3 information.

IN THE ELECTRONIC BUSINESS CARDS DIALOG BOX

Shortcut Keys	Assigned Action
ALT+A	Open the Add list.
ALT+B	Select text in Label box when the field with a label assigned is selected.
ALT+C	Open the Add Card Picture dialog box.
ALT+E	Place cursor at beginning of Edit box.
ALT+F	Select the Fields box.
ALT+G	Select the Image Align drop-down list.
ALT+K, then ENTER	Select color palette for background.
ALT+L	Select Layout drop-down list.
ALT+R	Remove a selected field from the Fields box.

TASKS

Shortcut Keys	Assigned Action
ALT+F2	Show or hide the To-Do Bar.
ALT+C	Accept a task request.

ALT+D	Decline a task request.
CTRL+E	Find a task or other item.
CTRL+Y	Open the Go to Folder dialog box.
CTRL+N	Create a new task (when in Tasks).
CTRL+SHIFT+K	Create a new task (from any Outlook view).
CTRL+SHIFT+U	Create a new task request.
CTRL+O	Open selected item.
CTRL+P	Print selected item.
CTRL+A	Select all items.
CTRL+D	Delete selected item.
CTRL+F	Forward a task as an attachment.
SHIFT+TAB	Switch between the Navigation Pane, Tasks list, and To-Do Bar.
CTRL+J	Open selected item as a Journal item.
CTRL+Z	Undo last action.
INSERT	Flag an item or mark complete.

FORMAT TEXT

Shortcut Keys	Assigned Action
ALT+O	Display the Format menu.
CTRL+SHIFT+P	Display the Font dialog box.
SHIFT+F3	Switch case (with text selected).
CTRL+SHIFT+K	Format letters as small capitals.
CTRL+B	Make letters bold.
CTRL+SHIFT+L	Add bullets.
CTRL+I	Make letters italic.
CTRL+T	Increase indent.
CTRL+SHIFT+T	Decrease indent.

CTRL+L	Left align.
CTRL+E	Center.
CTRL+U	Underline.
CTRL+] or CTRL+SHIFT+>	Increase font size.
CTRL+[or CTRL+SHIFT+<	Decrease font size.
CTRL+X or SHIFT+DELETE	Cut.
CTRL+C or CTRL+INSERT **Note CTRL+INSERT is not available in the Reading Pane.**	Copy.
CTRL+V or SHIFT+INSERT	Paste.
CTRL+SHIFT+Z or CTRL+SPACEBAR	Clear formatting.
CTRL+SHIFT+H	Delete the next word.
CTRL+SHIFT+J	Stretch a paragraph to fit between the margins.
CTRL+SHIFT+S	Apply styles.
CTRL+T	Create a hanging indent.
CTRL+K	Insert a hyperlink.
CTRL+L	Left align a paragraph.
CTRL+R	Right align a paragraph.
CTRL+SHIFT+T	Reduce a hanging indent.
CTRL+Q	Remove paragraph formatting.

ADD WEB INFORMATION TO ITEMS

Shortcut Keys	Assigned Action
Hold down CTRL and click the mouse button.	Edit a URL in the body of an item.
Hold down SHIFT and click the mouse button.	Specify a Web browser.
CTRL+K	Insert a hyperlink.

PRINT PREVIEW

Shortcut Keys	Assigned Action
Press ALT+F and then press V	Open Print Preview.
To print an item in an open window, press ALT+F, press W, and then press V	
ALT+P	Print a print preview.
ALT+S or ALT+U	Open Page Setup from Print Preview.
ALT+Z	Zoom.
ALT+C	Close Print Preview.

SEND/RECEIVE

Shortcut Keys	Assigned Action
F9	Start a send/receive for all defined Send/Receive groups with Include this group in Send/Receive (F9) selected. This can include headers, full items, specified folders, items less than a specific size, or any combination that you define.
SHIFT+F9	Start a send/receive for the current folder, retrieving full items (header, item, and any attachments).
CTRL+M	Start a send/receive.
CTRL+ALT+S	Define Send/Receive groups.

VISUAL BASIC EDITOR

Shortcut Keys	Assigned Action
ALT+F11	Open Visual Basic Editor.

Macros

Shortcut Keys	Assigned Action
ALT+F8	Play macro.

FORMS

Shortcut Keys	Assigned Action
CTRL+ALT+SHIFT+F12	Save Form Design.
CTRL+SHIFT+F11	Save Form Data.

Click in an InfoPath folder, and then CTRL+N.	Create a new Microsoft Office InfoPath form.

VIEWS

Table view - General use

Shortcut Keys	Assigned Action
ENTER	Open an item.
CTRL+A	Select all items.
PAGE DOWN	Go to the item at the bottom of the screen.
PAGE UP	Go to the item at the top of the screen.
SHIFT+UP ARROW or SHIFT+DOWN ARROW, respectively	Extend or reduce the selected items by one item.
CTRL+UP ARROW or CTRL+DOWN ARROW, respectively	Go to the next or previous item without extending the selection.
CTRL+SPACEBAR	Select or cancel selection of the active item.
F5	Refresh view.

With a group selected

Shortcut Keys	Assigned Action
CTRL+SHIFT+PLUS SIGN	Expand all groups.
CTRL+MINUS SIGN	Collapse the group.
SHIFT+PLUS SIGN	Expand a single selected group.
MINUS SIGN	Collapse a single selected group.
UP ARROW	Select the previous group.
DOWN ARROW	Select the next group.
HOME	Select the first group.
END	Select the last group.
RIGHT ARROW	Select the first item on screen in an expanded group or the first item off screen to the right.

All groups

Shortcut Keys	Assigned Action
CTRL+MINUS SIGN	Collapse all groups.
CTRL+SHIFT+PLUS SIGN	Expand all groups.

CALENDAR DAY/WEEK/MONTH VIEW

All three

Shortcut Keys	Assigned Action
ALT+key for number of days	View from 1 through 9 days.
ALT+0 (ZERO)	View 10 days.
ALT+MINUS SIGN	Switch to weeks.
ALT+=	Switch to months.
CTRL+TAB or F6	Move between Calendar, TaskPad, and the Folder List.
SHIFT+TAB	Select the previous appointment.
LEFT ARROW	Go to the previous day.
RIGHT ARROW	Go to the next day.
ALT+DOWN ARROW	Go to the same day in the next week.
ALT+UP ARROW	Go to the same day in the previous week.

DAY VIEW

Shortcut Keys	Assigned Action
HOME	Select the time that begins your work day.
END	Select the time that ends your work day.
UP ARROW	Select the previous block of time.
DOWN ARROW	Select the next block of time.
PAGE UP	Select the block of time at the top of the screen.
PAGE DOWN	Select the block of time at the bottom of the screen.

SHIFT+UP ARROW or SHIFT+DOWN ARROW, respectively	Extend or reduce the selected time.
With the cursor in the appointment, ALT+UP ARROW or ALT+DOWN ARROW, respectively	Move an appointment up or down.
With the cursor in the appointment, ALT+SHIFT+UP ARROW or ALT+SHIFT+DOWN ARROW, respectively	Change an appointment's start or end time.
ALT+DOWN ARROW	Move selected item to the same day in the next week.
ALT+UP ARROW	Move selected item to the same day in the previous week.

WEEK VIEW

Shortcut Keys	Assigned Action
HOME	Go to the start of work hours for the selected day.
END	Go to the end of work hours for the selected day.
PAGE UP	Go up one page view in the selected day.
PAGE DOWN	Go down one page view in the selected day.
ALT+UP ARROW, ALT+DOWN ARROW, ALT+LEFT ARROW, or ALT+RIGHT ARROW, respectively	Move the appointment up, down, left, or right.
SHIFT+LEFT ARROW, SHIFT+RIGHT ARROW, SHIFT+UP ARROW, or SHIFT+DOWN ARROW; or SHIFT+HOME or SHIFT+END	Change the duration of the selected block of time.

MONTH VIEW

Shortcut Keys	Assigned Action
HOME	Go to the first day of the week.
PAGE UP	Go to the same day of the week in the previous page.
PAGE DOWN	Go to the same day of the week in the next page.

DATE NAVIGATOR

Shortcut Keys	Assigned Action
ALT+HOME	Go to the first day of the current week.
ALT+END	Go to the last day of the current week.
ALT+UP ARROW	Go to the same day in the previous week.
ALT+DOWN ARROW	Go to the same day in the next week.

BUSINESS CARDS VIEW OR ADDRESS CARDS VIEW

General use

Shortcut Keys	Assigned Action
One or more letters of the name that the card is filed under or the name of the field that you are sorting by	Select a specific card in the list.
UP ARROW	Select the previous card.
DOWN ARROW	Select the next card.
HOME	Select the first card in the list.
END	Select the last card in the list.
PAGE UP	Select the first card on the current page.
PAGE DOWN	Select the first card on the next page.
RIGHT ARROW	Select the closest card in the next column.
LEFT ARROW	Select the closest card in the previous column.
CTRL+SPACEBAR	Select or cancel selection of the active card.
SHIFT+UP ARROW	Extend the selection to the previous card and cancel selection of cards after the starting point.
SHIFT+DOWN ARROW	Extend the selection to the next card and cancel selection of cards before the starting point.
CTRL+SHIFT+UP ARROW	Extend the selection to the previous card, regardless of the starting point.
CTRL+SHIFT+DOWN ARROW	Extend the selection to the next card, regardless

	of the starting point.
SHIFT+HOME	Extend the selection to the first card in the list.
SHIFT+END	Extend the selection to the last card in the list.
SHIFT+PAGE UP	Extend the selection to the first card on the previous page.
SHIFT+PAGE DOWN	Extend the selection to the last card on the last page.

Move between fields in an open card

To use the following keys, make sure a field in a card is selected. To select a field when a card is selected, click the field or press F2.

Shortcut Keys	Assigned Action
TAB	Move to the next field and, from the last field of a card, move to the first field in the next card.
SHIFT+TAB	Move to the previous field and, from the first field of a card, move to the last field in the previous card.
ENTER	Move to the next field, or add a line to a multiline field.
SHIFT+ENTER	Move to the previous field without leaving the active card.
F2	Display the insertion point in the active field to edit text.

Move between characters in a field

To use the following keys, make sure a field in a card is selected. To select a field when a card is selected, click the field or press F2.

Shortcut Keys	Assigned Action
ENTER	Add a line in a multiline field.
HOME	Move to the beginning of a line.
END	Move to the end of a line.
PAGE UP	Move to the beginning of a multiline field.
PAGE DOWN	Move to the end of a multiline field.
UP ARROW	Move to the previous line in a multiline field.

DOWN ARROW	Move to the next line in a multiline field.
LEFT ARROW	Move to the previous character in a field.
RIGHT ARROW	Move to the next character in a field.

TIMELINE VIEW (TASKS OR JOURNAL)

Following short cuts are applicable only when an item is selected in Tasks or Journal components of Microsoft Office Outlook 2013.

Shortcut Keys	Assigned Action
LEFT ARROW	Select the previous item.
RIGHT ARROW	Select the next item.
SHIFT+LEFT ARROW	Multi-Select. Selects adjacent items.
SHIFT+RIGHT ARROW	Multi-Select. Selects adjacent items.
CTRL+LEFT ARROW+SPACEBAR	Multi-Select. Selects several nonadjacent items.
CTRL+RIGHT ARROW+SPACEBAR	Multi-Select. Selects several nonadjacent items.
ENTER	Open the selected items.
PAGE UP	Display the items one screen above the items on screen.
PAGE DOWN	Display the items one screen below the items on screen.
HOME	Select the first item on the timeline (if items are not grouped) or the first item in the group.
END	Select the last item on the timeline (if items are not grouped) or the last item in the group.
CTRL+HOME	Display (without selecting) the first item on the timeline (if items are not grouped) or the first item in the group.
CTRL+END	Display (without selecting) the last item on the timeline (if items are not grouped) or the last item in the group.

Following short cuts are applicable only when a group is selected in Tasks or Journal components of Microsoft Office Outlook 2013.

Shortcut Keys	Assigned Action
ENTER or RIGHT ARROW	Expand the group.
ENTER or LEFT ARROW	Collapse the group.
UP ARROW	Select the previous group.
DOWN ARROW	Select the next group.
HOME	Select the first group on the timeline.
END	Select the last group on the timeline.
RIGHT ARROW	Select the first item on screen in an expanded group or the first item off screen to the right.

Following short cuts are applicable only when a unit of time on the time scale for days is selected in Tasks or Journal components of Microsoft Office Outlook 2013.

Shortcut Keys	Assigned Action
RIGHT ARROW	Move forward in increments of time that are the same as those shown on the time scale.
LEFT ARROW	Move back in increments of time that are the same as those shown on the time scale.
SHIFT+TAB	When the lower time scale is selected, select the upper time scale.
TAB	When the upper time scale is selected, select the lower time scale.
	When the lower time scale is selected, select the first item on screen or the first group on screen if items are grouped.

This concludes this section on Microsoft Outlook shortcut keys. Please note that this is not an exhaustive list of different possible functions. There are many more unexplored options that you may want to discover. In case you come across such functions do let me know and I shall update this eBook and send it back to you free of cost.

HOW TO CREATE APPLICATION HOTKEY FOR MS-OUTLOOK?

Having read above sections I am sure you would have gained a lot of insight into different shortcuts of Microsoft Outlook program. I am sure that many of you might be wondering if you could assign a Hotkey to invoke a windows application such that it starts automatically (without manually launching the application following standard method) on pressing the hotkey sequence. For the benefit of all, including those who are wondering the method of assigning shortcut to Application for quick startup and also those who haven't been wondering here comes a quick shortcut way to assign your custom hotkey to just about any Windows based application...

1. Create a shortcut to your favorite application program
   - ➤ Open the folder or directory that contains the program you wish to create a shortcut for.
   - ➤ Right-click on the program and click **Create Shortcut**.
   - ➤ This will create a shortcut named "Shortcut to <your program>" in the directory you are currently in. If you wish to rename this shortcut, right-click the file and click rename.
2. Once the shortcut is created, you should copy it on the desktop. It will also let you have quick access to the application manually, should you forget the assigned hot key.
3. Assign a shortcut key to that Windows shortcut: Once the shortcut has been created to assign a shortcut key to that Windows shortcut follow the below steps.

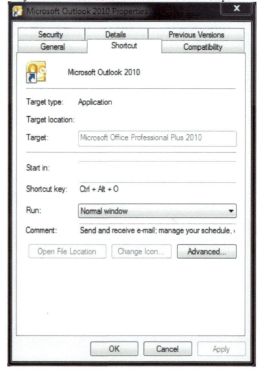

Figure 1

- ➤ Open shortcut properties of the application shortcut you pasted on desktop in previous step. To open shortcut properties **Right-click** the shortcut and click **Properties**.
- ➤ Click the Shortcut tab.

- ➤ Click in the Shortcut key box and press a letter. For instance, **Ctrl + Alt + O**
- ➤ Click the Apply button
- ➤ Click the Ok button to close the shortcut properties window
4. Launch the application using shortcuts keys. In our example **Ctrl + Alt + O**

CONCLUDING WORDS

You may get your work done on a computer without knowing even a single shortcut key. However, such work would cost you time and result in poor performance, and productivity. Moreover, certain repetitive tasks could make your work a tedious one. Computer shortcuts therefore, have an important role to play in quickly introducing in productivity in the work you do.

I hope you would find this small compilation of useful shortcuts for Microsoft Outlook handy specially when in need of performing repetitive task. If you are able to recall and use even 50 percent of the shortcuts it is likely to double your productivity with Microsoft office – Outlook application.

Last but not least, I have taken lot of efforts to make sure the information presented here is accurate however, should you feel that a particular information or shortcut key is not working for you it could be due to specific brand of your computer. However, I would welcome your suggestions and inputs in this regard. When reporting an error do mention the environment your are working in including hardware, make, model, software, and operating system to help me recreate the environment and test the issue.

Rapid Collaborating!!!